GW01607666

The Not Another Book of Old Photographs Book

A Welsh hillside shepherd c. 1906

HONEYSETT

The Not Another Book of Old Photographs Book

with a preface by The Unknown Social Historian

EYRE METHUEN · LONDON

First published in 1981
by Eyre Methuen Ltd
11 New Fetter Lane, London EC4P 4EE

ISBN 0 413 48590 0

Printed in Great Britain
by Fletcher & Son Ltd
Norwich, Norfolk

Preface

This is not another book of old photographs.
It is an amazing compilation of images evocative of a past our grandparents and great-grandparents might once have half recalled or might have denied all knowledge of.

Caveat emptor.

The Unknown Social Historian

Two porters arriving to work at Covent Garden Market

Women harvesting in field

NESTLE'S
MILK
CLAPHAM
BATTERSEA
THE RED STAR OMNIBUS
CO

A development of the stage coach, one of the first double-decker omnibuses

A cow bladder balloon seller

Tree felling in Oxfordshire

Lady Cragthorn-Croak and housemaid

Children collecting firewood

South Coast beach scene: early 1900's

A country barber

Two London housewives

City bank interior, 1886

GRUBS
&
SOAP

A circus parade in Wandsworth

Scottish bricklayer and hod-carrier

Waggoner about to cross the ford at Ilchester

The Bakewell to Baslow Annual Cycle Race, 1898

Poor Quarter, London 1881

Barges on the Trent and Mersey Canal

HERBERT

A young road-sweeper, c. 1900

Herring curers at Aberdour

Two flower sellers (one with hay fever)

The Scraggley-Morton steam guillotine of 1910

Firemen with horse-drawn steam pump

ONDON
E BRIGADE

Milking cows in the field

A group of roadmenders in Streatham

Young girls with a goat cart

Jack Sproat, rabbit catcher

BRISKET BROS.
HIGH CLASS FAMILY BUTCHER
72

Two High Street shops

J. Fuller, a seaside Punch and Judy man, at home

Cattle market in Llanfyllin

An early tipper truck

Shearing sheep in Dorset

Dipping sheep in Somerset

Women labourers taking their meal break

A knife grinder
and customer

Refreshment stop for carters and van drivers

CRUDWORTH
BAKERY
9A ESSEX
METROPOLITAN DRINKING
FOUNTAIN ASSOCIATION
TEAS

The Royal mouse catcher, Buckingham Palace 1894

A family of charcoal burners in the New Forest

MAX LOAD
4 MEN
8 MOLES

uilding one of London's underground railways in the 1860's

Head cooper at Bung's brewery, Lambeth

Two watermen

Harrowing in Sussex with a team of oxen

Some of London's cockneys on their annual nit-picking holiday in Kent

Funeral procession, Streatham, 1903

Middle-class bathtime

Working-class bathtime

Head gardener and assistant at Tickhill Manor, Northamptonshire

Women
collecting water
from the village pump

Morning delivery, Lambeth

Gypsies, somewhere in Hampshire, 1904

Clergymen meeting at the Rectory, South Allsop, 1901